BATTERSEA PARK

BATTERSEA PARK

Jennifer Ullman

PUBLISHED BY THE FRIENDS OF BATTERSEA PARK : 2016

This book is dedicated to my husband John,
who shared with me the adventure of living
in Battersea Park for more than a decade and
who continues to be my companion on life's
best adventures. Thank you for your patience,
understanding and, most of all, your love.

Battersea Park by Jennifer Ullman
Published in 2016
by the Friends of Battersea Park

Designed and brought to press by John Commander
Printed and bound by JNV Print Ltd, Essex CO6 4PX

A CIP record for this book
is available from the British Library

ISBN 978-0-9520981-1-9

www.batterseapark.org

Foreword

This book brings alive the features within Battersea Park. It explains what those behind the development of the Park were trying to achieve, from its beginnings in the mid-19th century to the Festival of Britain in the mid-20th century. It also explains the thinking behind the restoration of the Park, which was completed early this century.

The Friends of Battersea Park published a small volume, *Battersea Park: An Illustrated History,* in 1993. Its aim was 'to inform and amuse' and there can be no doubt that it did so delightfully. However, the Friends have been keen for some time to bring the story up to date.

Since 1993, much has changed. The large-scale restoration programme ran from 1998 to 2004, funded by Wandsworth Council and the Heritage Lottery Fund. The Winter Garden, created by Dan Pearson, was opened in 2011. A year later, the Old English Garden was transformed by Sarah Price.

The Friends have been fortunate that Jennifer Ullman, Chief Parks Officer from 2005 to 2008 who arrived in the Park in 1998 to help with the restoration, agreed to update our history. It was quickly decided that, rather than simply adding to the 1993 volume, it would be better if she were to write a new book, which might last another twenty years. The Friends are extremely grateful to Jennifer and all those who have given so much time and enthusiasm to bringing the book to completion and particularly to the John Murray Charitable Trust for a generous grant towards publication.

Battersea Park has always been subject to change. In October 2015, management of the Park transferred to a newly created Staff Mutual. Larger changes mark the landscape around the Park: buildings are rising in Nine Elms, including on the Battersea Power Station site, bringing many new local residents.

The Friends of Battersea Park was founded in 1988 to help maintain and improve the Park as an oasis of tranquillity, natural beauty and recreation. These objectives will not change. Most of all, the Friends want to pay tribute to all those who work in the Park to look after its plants, wildlife and fabric so that it continues to give so much pleasure to so many people.

FRANCES RADCLIFFE
Chairman, Friends of Battersea Park   May 2016

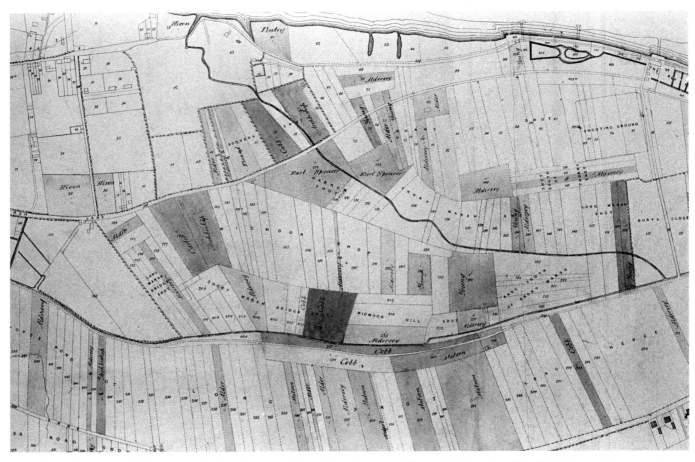

Part of Battersea Fields prior to the development of the Park with some 360 smallholding plots. The Red House *is located at top right of the above plan.*

Beginnings

Victorian London was a dynamic and swiftly changing place. The industrial revolution brought thousands of workers to the city, swelling the population. At the same time, the government embarked on massive modernisation programmes, building new roads and bridges, and creating whole neighbourhoods. Nothing seemed impossible to Victorians with vision, who wanted a shining new city of wealth and modern prosperity.

In the early 1800s Battersea Fields was a series of smallholdings on what had previously been common land. Cattle were grazed there in the winter, and in the summer the fields were used for growing hay and vegetables. To one side was the Red House, an inn that attracted day-trippers arriving by steamboat and which,

The Red House

by night, had an unsavoury reputation. The fairs that were held on the Fields on Sundays were renowned for their shady characters, boxing contests and dog fights. One writer claimed that 'if ever there was a place out of Hell that surpassed Sodom and Gomorrah in ungodliness and abomination, this was it.'

WILLIAM HEATH: *The Field of Battersea*

Wellington in monk's robes with rosary fires wide in the direction of Winchelsea who has made himself very thin and fires into the air.

Wellington: *I used to be a good shot, but have been out of practice for some years.*

Winchelsea: *I'll make myself up small. God if he should hit me I might be tainted with some of his Popery. Won't give him more than one chance.*

THE FIELD OF BATTERSEA

Battersea Fields was the venue for a famous duel between the then Prime Minister, the Duke of Wellington, and the 10th Earl of Winchelsea on 21 March 1829. The matter of honour at stake was Catholics' rights, which had been removed a couple of centuries earlier. Wellington had successfully pushed through the Catholic Emancipation Act, which restored nearly full civil rights to Catholics in the UK and Ireland. Winchelsea disagreed, stating that the Act was 'an insidious design for the infringement of our liberties and the introduction of Popery into every department of the State'. Wellington responded by challenging him to a duel, which took place near the infamous Red House, close to what is now the Chelsea Gate entrance to the Park. When the time came to fire, the Earl did not raise his arm and the Duke shot wide. Honour was served, Winchelsea apologised and both came away unscathed.

In 1846, the Vicar of Battersea, Rev. the Hon. Robert Eden, argued forcefully that a park was needed to solve the problem of disreputable behaviour in Battersea Fields, which he attributed to the lack of any pastime other than the pub for workers' leisure hours on Sundays:

> 'Many of these persons would become orderly if pains were taken to provide for them healthful recreation [which will] promote social and domestic happiness, [and] implant feelings which are now deadened by dirt, by drink and by discomfort'.

Another supporter of reform for Battersea Fields was Thomas Cubitt, the great developer of Belgravia, who first conceived the idea of a bridge across the Thames, connecting the handsome neighbourhoods of Pimlico and Belgravia that he was building to a newly created residential area and park on Battersea Fields. In 1843 he made a proposal to the Royal Commission of Metropolitan Improvements but was not prepared to pay for the construction of the park himself. The Commission turned to their architect, James Pennethorne, for an initial design and costing, with a third of the land to be dedicated to new housing to pay for the construction of a park.

James Pennethorne, 1865

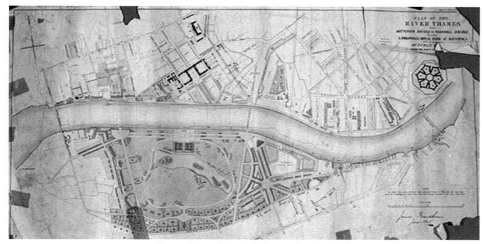

Pennethorne's initial design for the Park

9

Pennethorne sketched out the bones of what we see in the Park today: a circular carriage drive, lake and riverside promenade, but with villas within the perimeter of the Park. Convinced that the scheme would make a profit, the Commissioners approved the proposal and in 1846 an Act of Parliament was passed that authorised the Commissioners of Woods and Forests to borrow £200,000 for making the park and £120,000 for the construction of Chelsea Bridge.

Pennethorne set about securing the land from the smallholders. This proved a protracted and expensive process, as once the decision to create a park was made public, many smallholders held out for as much as ten times the value of the land. With the original budget blown before work had begun, the government voted a rescue package of additional funds in 1854.

If a park were to be created now on Battersea Fields as it was in 1854, it would look very different from what Pennethorne proposed. Today, designers would work with the low-lying marshy wetland by the river, creating a landscape of reeds, rushes and meadows. They would look to enhance the natural landscape features for biodiversity and conservation and they would incorporate the tidal fluctuation of the Thames. The Victorian ethos was markedly different. Pennethorne's design dramatically changed the existing topography of Battersea Fields and created an entirely new landscape with raised contours, artificial lakes and cascades, formal carriage drives and promenades. The natural landscape was to be superseded by an artificial ornamental landscape designed to impress and delight.

As work began, the first priority was to raise the ground level by about 24 feet (7 metres) as much of the land was prone to flooding. As many as twenty barges a day brought soil from the excavation of the Victoria Docks in east London; in total, over a million tonnes of soil arrived on site.

In 1856, rebutting concerns over expenditure, Pennethorne assured the First Commissioner of Works, Sir Benjamin Hall, that:

'In a few years, after the plantations shall have formed, there will probably not be a Park near London presenting more attractions of Scenery or more sources for the enjoyment and recreation of the Public than Battersea Park – and the locality alto-

John Gibson (1815-1872)
first Superintendent of the Park

gether, instead of being (as would have been the case) a hot bed of malaria, fever and crime, will be, as I firmly believe, a Suburb worthy in every respect of the West End of London'.

Hall was unimpressed and when Pennethorne refused to accept responsibility for overspending on the original budget, relieved him of further control of the project.

With the initial layout complete, responsibility for further developing the Park was given to John Gibson, the Park's first Superintendent. A talented horticulturalist, Gibson had worked on the Duke of Devonshire's Chatsworth Estate under Joseph Paxton. This was the era of the great plant hunters, when men went to India, China and the Americas to search for rare and highly prized horticultural specimens. Sent to India to hunt for orchids in 1835, when he was only twenty, Gibson arrived at the Botanic Garden in Calcutta where he is described as running around like an excited schoolboy, clapping his hands with joy at the plants that he saw. His three-month journey into the Khosea Hills was dangerous but highly successful: he was able to send back to Britain a rich and exciting haul of horticultural wonders, including more than eighty entirely unknown orchids. Writing to Paxton, Gibson stated, 'I never saw, nor could I believe that there was such a fertile place under the Heavens… and I think the whole of the plants are entirely new to the European collections'.

Gibson came to Battersea Park from Victoria Park in east London, where he had previously worked with Pennethorne, bringing with him a rich knowledge of exotic plants and excellent connections with nurserymen. When Battersea Park opened in 1858, it was far from complete and Gibson set about creating a landscape of rich botanical wonders, using land contour and planting to create a sense of enclosure, with shrubberies lining the perimeter boundaries and entrances, and serpentine paths opening out onto broad, open, meadow-like playing fields. Through his contacts, Gibson sourced rare and unusual plants, viewing the entire Park as a canvas for botanical wonders. Specimen trees were put on mounds to make them look impressive. A favoured trick was to lead the visitor through shady and secluded pathways that opened up to sudden vistas, striking landscape features and colourful garden areas.

Battersea Park in 1858 shortly after opening

The most impressive of these spectacles was the Subtropical Garden, where Gibson displayed a new style of bedding, largely his own creation. Nestled in a high-sided dell by the lake and protected from winds by a shelterbelt of trees, the Subtropical Garden was a stunning display of tender and exotic plants never before seen in a public garden in the United Kingdom. The island planting beds were set into lawn and had rubble underneath the soil to soak up the heat of the sun during the day and disperse heat at night to keep the plants warm.

Large-leaved palms, bananas, aralias and dracaenas chosen for their dramatic and contrasting foliage astonished and delighted visitors. Within a few years, Gibson

13

had also perfected carpet bedding, the intricate creation of patterns including words or symbols, by planting low-growing plants closely packed together.

It is difficult for us today to understand just how surprising the Subtropical Garden must have been for first-time visitors, with its enormous leaves, giant palm fronds and the jostling, vivid colours of the tropical bedding plants. Now, even if we have never journeyed to exotic places, we know what they look like. We see them in print and on television in vivid colour when presenters guide us through rainforests. For visitors to the Subtropical Garden in 1864, who would have only read about such places and seen illustrations in black and white, it must have been an amazing experience.

Gibson had other surprises in store. After an interlude of tranquillity walking from the Subtropical Garden between the lake and Ladies Pond (so called for the women-only ice skating that took place there), the enclosed path passed over a rustic bridge made of huge, rough-hewn logs. This was the first clue to visitors that

The Cascades from early postcards

they had left behind the tranquil shores of England and entered a dramatic alpine wonderland. Continuing past a raised bulwark of earth, visitors rounded a corner to see towering above them striking cascades of water, flowing into basins and over ledges on the side of a cliff rock face. These were the Cascades, artfully made in 1873 by James Pulham & Son to replicate natural rock. Planted by Gibson with scrambling clematis and craggy pine trees, the Cascades were meant to look as impressive as something that might have been seen on a postcard from Switzerland.

Such design tricks are direct precursors of what we now encounter at visitor attractions such as theme parks. Gibson put his visitors on a carefully constructed journey, shaping all elements of their experience as they moved from space to space, using soothing interludes, hints of excitements ahead, and then suddenly revealing a striking landscape feature.

Gibson installed James Pulham's artificial rocks or 'Pulhamite' in several places in the Park, each to add drama to a setting. In the American Ground, in the north-east corner of the Park, so called for its American species of plants, there was a large Pulhamite arch. In the deer enclosure, a raised knoll with craggy rocks implied that the visitor was far away from the flat, featureless London landscape. Outside the Italianate Pump House, then a purely functional building to pump water to the Cascades, a large outcrop of Pulhamite marked the entrance to the walkways leading to the Cascades

Throughout the Park, Gibson planted areas of bedding and used large swathes of perennials and flowering shrubs in the long borders along the edges of the lake to create visual beauty and interest. The Rosery Garden at the south-west corner welcomed visitors arriving from Queenstown Circus, leading them past arbours cloaked in roses to the water's edge where a dramatic view of the Cascades could be seen.

Lakeside Gunnera

Drinking Fountain

The Aviary

The Riverside proved to be problematic. Although Pennethorne had envisaged a wide promenade with a substantial granite riverside wall with inset benches, seasonal high water levels washed the raised earth away. Before the construction of the Thames Barrier in 1984, water would occasionally sweep across the Park during high tides. Elements of Pennethorne's original design were not achieved until the 1998–2004 restoration of the Park.

As the Park developed in the 19th century, lodges were built at Albert Gate, Rosery Gate and Sun Gate for Park staff. An elegant Refreshment House was built on North Carriage Drive and sports facilities were added.

Flooding at high tide c. 1900

The Refreshment House

From its first opening, the Park was a tremendous success. Gibson's horticultural innovations were written up widely in the press. Day-trippers arriving by steamboat pushed the visitor numbers up to a reported 50,000 on a Sunday. Large events were held on the open spaces, attracting over 100,000 people. As intended by its creators, Battersea Park became a place where people from all walks of life could come to spend their leisure hours, strolling around the paths, listening to the music, taking refreshment, boating on the lake or playing sport.

Tennis Court, Battersea Park.

BATTERSEA PARK
CHILDREN AND

LONDON LIFE.
BOATING BATTERSEA PARK.

23

Skating on Ladies' Pond, c1880

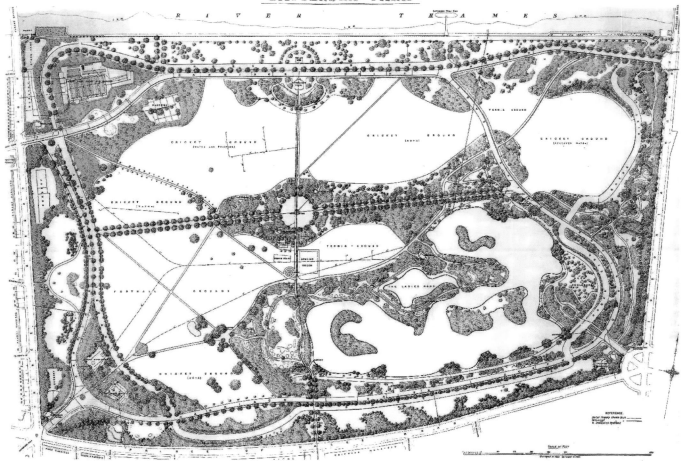

In 1889, the management of the Park passed to the newly formed London County Council (LCC), which managed parks all across London. Over subsequent years, the emphasis moved away from horticultural showmanship to a greater emphasis on sport. However, horticultural improvements continued to be made. In 1911, Lieutenant Colonel J. J. Sexby, then Superintendent of all LCC parks, created the Old English Garden in the north-west corner of the Park where some of the nurseries propagating plants for the Park were situated. Sexby put Old English Gardens, all similar in style, into a number of London parks. The walled Old English Garden at Battersea had a series of formal geometric beds around a central rectangular pool with water lilies. Box topiary gave structure, as did an arbour and arches with climbers. The planting was mainly roses and bedding. Over the years, a number of fountains have graced the pool, with the current fountain, a replica of the original, donated by the Friends of Battersea Park in 1999. The Old English Garden was to be the last new garden created for the Park before the outbreak of the First World War.

OLD GARDEN
BATTERSEA PARK LONDON

Into the 20th Century: the World Wars and beyond

In 2002 the payroll books for the Park staff from the late 1930s were discovered amongst cobwebs on a shelf in a shed. They contain some poignant entries, indicating those on the weekly log who left to fight in the Second World War.

> *Week ending 13 September 1939*
>
> ~~Pook, E J   Remarks: Military Duties~~
>
> ~~Ritchie, R   Remarks: Military Duties~~

The above entries have lines through them and do not appear in the following week.

> *Week ending 17 July 1940*
>
> Sturges, F.G, Annual leave. *Remarks:* 15th July 1940, Military Service
>
> *Week ending 6 November 1940*
>
> Humphreys, Assistant. *Remarks:* Joined the Navy 7/11/40

These names make real the impact of war on a park served by dozens of gardeners and keepers, as one by one they disappeared off to the services. The maintenance of garden areas ceased and sports fields were turned over to vegetable growing and gun emplacements.

Battersea Park joined in the effort to feed and defend the nation during both the First and Second World Wars, and both wars took their toll on the landscape in ways that can still be seen. The Park was vulnerable to bombing as it was surrounded by railway lines vital for transporting troops and supplying London with food, with important industrial sites nearby including Battersea Power Station and the Nine Elms Gasworks, both critical to keeping London going. During 1944 and 1945, seven V1 and V2 bombs fell in the Park, intended for these neighbouring targets, causing damage but no fatalities. One large bomb crater still exists on an island in the lake, and a substantial underground air-raid shelter remains near Prince of Wales Drive. Accessed by a small entrance with stairs leading down to a large, rectangular room, the shelter has hooks on the walls from which stretcher beds were suspended, stacking neighbour above neighbour as they sheltered from the bombs.

Allotment gardens in the Park

Entrance to the air-raid shelter

27

In both World Wars, huge areas were turned over to allotment gardens, allowing people to grow precious food to supplement the meagre rations. In the First World War, the Carriage Drives were surfaced to support military lorries bringing in troops for drills. During the Second World War, an anti-aircraft station was built over the croquet lawn. A piggery was established to help feed the surrounding population. A barrage balloon was sited in the Park and a large anti-aircraft gun emplacement manned by the Home Guard was established in the north-east corner where the running track is today.

The Park emerged from the Second World War a changed place. All the railings had been taken away to be melted down for the war effort. The ornamental gardens, other than the Old English Garden, had been lost and the shrubberies had become overgrown. Many parks suffered in similar ways, and contemporaries noted the negative effect of the railing removals and the loss of park keepers due to postwar austerity and budgetary cutbacks resulting in increased vandalism and antisocial behaviour

Despite its depleted condition, however, Battersea Park became the site of a renaissance in the arts and a great festival symbolising the rebirth of the nation after the long, bleak years of war. In 1948, the first in a series of major public open-air sculpture exhibitions was held in the Park on the area that had once been the Subtropical Garden and was then lawn. Organised by the LCC Parks Committee and the Arts Council, it was Patricia Strauss, a Labour politician and Chair of the LCC Parks Committee, who first came up with the idea, which she thought would prove popular and give publicity to the Council. It is likely that the success of this first exhibition led to Battersea Park being considered by the Labour government as one of the main venues for the Festival of Britain.

Elected in 1945, the Labour government was busy rebuilding and rehousing the nation. England's recovery from the war was slow. Rationing was still in place, winters were bitterly cold and coal was in short supply. Nationalisation was the new government initiative and the idea of boosting trade and morale through a celebration or festival on the anniversary of the 1851 Great Exhibition gained strength in Parliament.

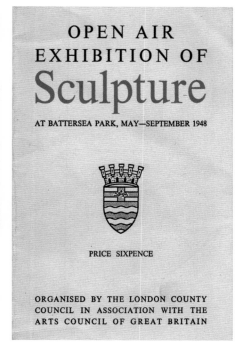

Private view day at the 1948 sculpture exhibition

In 1947, Gerald Barry was appointed Director-General of the Festival. He was determined that it would show 'the British contribution to civilisation past, present and future, in the arts, in science and technology and in industrial design. Moreover, he decided that it should be *FUN*. As well as various venues across the nation, the main Festival sites would be the London South Bank for arts, innovation and achievement, and Battersea Park for a pleasure garden in the spirit of previous famous London pleasure gardens, such as Vauxhall and Ranelagh. These had featured restaurants, theatrical performances and concerts as well as ornamental gardens. James Gardner was appointed to oversee the Battersea project. Originally a jewellery designer, he had worked on camouflage during the war and had moved on to designing exhibitions. According to the landscape designer Russell Page, who worked with him, Gardner 'understood well the possibilities of wood, glass, metal, plasterboard, paint and canvas.'

Gerald Barry

James Gardner

John Piper and Osbert Lancaster

Russell Page

Gardner, Page, the cartoonist Osbert Lancaster and the artist John Piper worked together to populate the Pleasure Gardens with fantastical, whimsical structures, mixing modern, Rococo, Georgian and Gothic architecture into a style that was christened 'English Picturesque'. Designed to last only a year and with building supplies restricted, the pavilions and landscape features were created out of cheap, ephemeral materials using many tricks of theatrical design.

Dozens of designers were brought in to work on different attractions within the site, all of which had to be allocated space and constructed. The winter of 1950–51 was long and wet. Seasonal tides brought the Thames over the Promenade, and the low-lying areas of the Park became waterlogged. The construction crews battled against a sea of mud, as Page and Gardner pushed to finish in time for planting. Labour strikes were rife and regularly disrupted work. However, the Festival was opened on time in May 1951 by King George VI.

The layout encompassed thirteen acres, with a circulation route from the river, where people would arrive from the South Bank by steam boat, then proceed down the Grand Vista, with its abundant fountains and arcades, to the tranquil central lawn area, now known as the Russell Page Garden, and then either back to the Riverside, with its refreshment kiosks and shops, or straight ahead into the children's zoo through an archway lined with aviaries and on to the fun fair.

Page designed the landscape and ornamental bedding that made the Festival so colourful. He decided that each structure should either have an area of formal bedding nearby or at least a window box of vibrant flowers. The Riverside refreshment kiosks were pale blue and white, so Page limited the flowers in this area to white, blue and yellow, planting 20,000 yellow tulips for the opening in May 1951. All the bedding was to be replaced continually throughout the Festival. As soon as an area had finished flowering, Page and his remarkable plant grower and advisor, E. R. Janes, just retired from the Suttons Seeds company, were ready with thousands of new plants to be put in place within hours of the previous plants being removed.

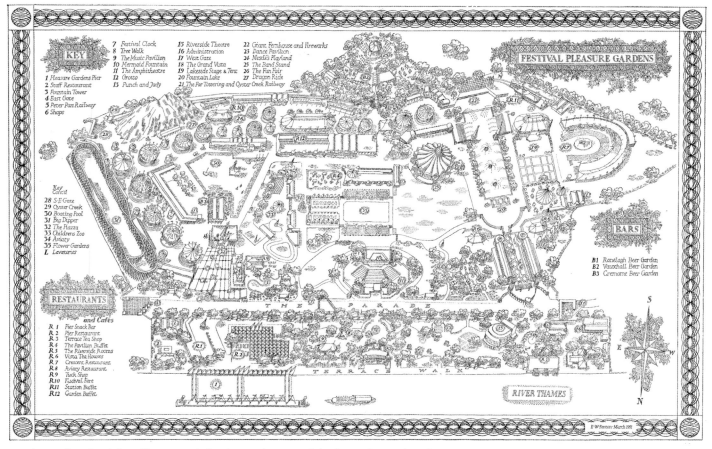

RIVER THAMES

E·W·Fenton·March 1951

As well as bedding, Page used shrubs and perennials throughout the site. Clearing the overgrown shrubbery banks that linked the Riverside to the lawn areas, Page created instant colour for the opening by bringing in mature salmon-pink rhododendrons from the famed Exbury Estate collection, from a group of plantings that had become overmature during the War. Filling the tired London clay with peat, Page produced the perfect environment for the rhododendrons that flourished during the Festival and then gradually died off over the years as the soil lost its acidity.

Page worked hard to get the visual effects of his planting right, writing:

'Usually in designing gardens you use colour in a setting of green hedges and grass and trees…. Here at Battersea, against acres of exuberant colour and fantastic painted arabesques, conventional planting or even solid patterns of flower colour could have entirely the wrong effect…. Finally I saw that I must mix my flower colours, plant in wide pools and drifts, let pale pinks overlap into clear lemon yellow, interplant orange with red-purple and use every device I could so that texture, colour, size and shape would combine to make all the flower plantings sparkle, shimmer and seem to move in contrast to the bright, flat and static surfaces of paint.'

THE PLEASURE GARDENS, FESTIVAL PLEASURE GARDENS, BATTERSEA.   VG 61.

The centrepiece of the Pleasure Gardens was the Grand Vista. Descending a wide staircase, visitors were greeted with a stunning view of pools and fountains surrounded by decorative obelisks and gothic towers. All the structures were painted red, black and ochre, vividly contrasting with the blue pools and pale concrete paving stones. At the end of the Vista was an enormous bamboo screen in the shape of the facade of the Great Exhibition, from which fireworks were let off nightly.

In addition to a concert hall, a theatre and restaurants, the main attractions included the Guinness Clock, a fantastical mechanical timepiece with an elaborate display of different characters every fifteen minutes, and the *Far Tottering and Oyster Creek Railway*, an equally fantastical narrow gauge railway designed by Roland Emmett, which took people on a circuit around part of the Park.

THE VISTA, FESTIVAL PLEASURE GARDENS, BATTERSEA. VG.81.

THE PARADE, FESTIVAL PLEASURE GARDENS

GUINNESS TIME

AT THE PLEASURE GARDENS

All the Guinness characters
   Whom everybody knows,
They've got a timely job to do
   That keeps them on their toes.

For every quarter-of-an-hour
   They help the clock to chime,
And they catch it from the keeper
   If they're late for Guinness Time.

HAVE A GLASS OF GUINNESS WHEN YOU'RE TIRED

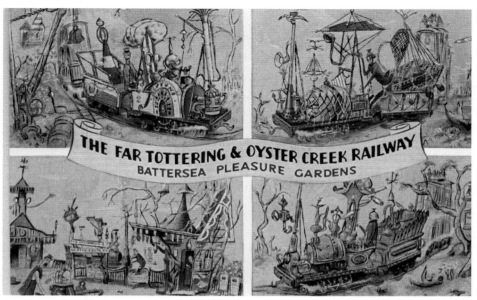

THE FAR TOTTERING & OYSTER CREEK RAILWAY

BATTERSEA PLEASURE GARDENS

"NELLIE" THE FAR TOTTERING AND OYSTER CREEK RAILWAY,
FESTIVAL GARDENS, FESTIVAL OF BRITAIN 1951.

The main sections of the Festival of Britain were officially closed at the end of September 1951. With the election of Churchill's Conservative government, which saw the Festival as part of Labour's overspending or 'squandermania', it was doomed. Exhibits were demolished and auctions held to disperse the contents. However, unlike the other sites, which were funded by the government, the company operating the Battersea site argued successfully to keep the gardens open for a further five years in an attempt to recover its original investment. The Battersea Pleasure Gardens continued but failed to recoup their funding and were finally closed and most of the structures dismantled. What remained were the landscape features, including the Grand Vista pools and fountains, the central lawn with its roses, and the children's zoo and fun fair.

The atmosphere of the Park and the fun fair are well summed up by the lyrics of Petula Clark's hit of 1954, *Meet Me in Battersea Park*:

> If you're a Londoner just like me,
> Meet me in Battersea Park.
> If you are young or you'd like to be,
> Meet me in Battersea Park.
> We'll stroll along by the riverside in sunshine or after it's dark.
> There's music and dancing, a place for romancing,
> So meet me in Battersea Park.
>
> See the people riding on the roundabouts and swings
> Children so delighted at the puppets on the strings
> Chair-o-planes a-whirling as they fly through the air
> Take a holiday, have a jolly day, come to the fair
>
> ... So meet me in Battersea, wonderful Battersea !
> Meet me in Battersea Park !

There are several films of the Battersea Park fun fair on the internet that vividly bring to life the swirling rides, jostling crowds, candyfloss sellers and flashing lights that were symbolic of this popular London attraction for more than twenty years. At the centre of the fun fair was the gigantic rollercoaster, the Big Dipper. It was this colossus that brought the end of the fun fair when, in May 1972, the open carriages detached from the haulage rope as they climbed towards the top of the ride and rolled backwards, killing five people and injuring thirteen others. The tragedy remains the worst in the history of fun fairs.

The fun fair site was cleared and subsequently hosted 'A Salute to British Genius', a temporary exhibition covering British achievements in the arts and sciences, which was visited by the Queen as part of her Silver Jubilee celebrations in

May 1977. The site remained after the exhibition ended, and the fenced area of tarmac and grass, now known as the Battersea Park Events Arena, hosts major events for London attended by many thousands of people every year.

The children's zoo was enlarged in the 1980s to cover four acres with an expanded animal range that included monkeys and a new reptile house. Hugely popular with the public, there was an outcry when Wandsworth Council threatened to close it in 2003. The zoo was then leased by Carol and Roger Heap, who built on the previous animal collection, participating in conservation programmes for endangered species and featuring many domestic and exotic species with the mission to inspire visitors to protect and conserve the earth for the animals' wild relatives.

Another late-20th-century addition to the Park was the establishment in1972 of a horticultural therapy garden near the Athletics Track. This was the first demonstration garden in the UK specifically created for people with a disability. Originally founded by the Disabled Living Foundation, the gardening service was taken over in the mid-1980s by the Society for Horticultural Therapy and Rural Training, now known as Thrive, which has expanded to garden other areas of the Park including the Herb Garden in the Staff Yard and the Old English Garden. Thrive is a national charity that works to help people with disabilities or mental health issues to transform their lives through gardening. A new building for the site by architects Pedder & Scampton, with a landscape by award-winning designer Sarah Price, opened in 2014.

One of the last acts of the Greater London Council was to authorise the building of a Peace Pagoda in Battersea Park. More than fifty monks, nuns and volunteers worked to construct the Pagoda, donated by Nipponzan Myohoji, a Japanese order of Buddhist monks, who construct peace pagodas around the world to promote world peace. Since 1985, the Reverend Gyoro Nagase (seen above), one of the original number, has remained in the Park, tending to the Pagoda and the small temple that was constructed in one of the service huts of the Festival of Britain, adjacent to the Grand Vista.

Restoration

The years 1990 to 2015 were a period of new beginnings for the Park, with a series of projects that transformed the tired landscape and recreated lost historic features.

From 1965 to1986, the Park was run by the Greater London Council (GLC). The historic garden features were largely lost and the Park had developed a reputation for being unsafe. In 1986, the GLC was dissolved and responsibilty for the Park was handed over to Wandsworth Council. From the beginning, the council sought to make improvements, erecting perimeter railings to enable the Park to be secured at night, installing a Victorian-style bandstand, adding new sports facilities and extending the children's zoo. To improve safety, the council also established its own police force, the Parks Police, which was based in the Park twenty-four hours a day.

Council landscape architect Jacqueline McCabe researched the history of the Park and suggested restoring some of its original features. At her instigation, pioneering work in the management of urban lakes saw the introduction in 1993 of new geese control fencing in the lake margins, offering the opportunity to replant the lakeside areas without the plants being stripped by geese. Perennial borders were planted and hoop-topped railings installed to recreate the Victorian appearance of the area around the Ladies Pond. This early work set out a vision of what could be achieved by restoring the original design intention of part of the Park, and prompted the council to aspire to further improvement projects.

In 1994, the Heritage Lottery Fund was established to make a lasting difference to heritage, people and communities across the UK. Wandsworth Council was an early applicant for funding to restore the Park and was awarded £6.9 million in 1998. The council committed a further £3.4 million to the project, making it one of the largest park restorations in the country. Funds were focused on re-establishing the main Victorian features and the landscape of the Festival of Britain Pleasure Gardens. Spanning five years, the work was divided into phases to minimise disruption to the Park and its users.

The Friends of Battersea Park, a charity formed by local residents, became a key partner in the improvement of the Park at this time, working with the council to ensure that Park users' interests were best served. The Friends, founded in 1988, had been early champions of the history of the Park, planting a palm tree in the area of the lost Subtropical Garden to indicate the historic landscape that had once been there.

The first phase of the restoration focused on buildings. On the team of consultants enlisted by the council to design the restoration was Rod McAllister, a young architect who designed the Boathouse and the Fountain Pump House and lavatories. The Boathouse, a stunning wood and metal structure, echoes the vernacular of a traditional boathouse but with modern structural elements, including a massive sliding barn door. McAllister chose materials that would not need painting or staining in the future, including the brilliant copper roof that aged

Fountain Pumphouse toilets

to verdigris over the first year of the Boathouse's life. The design won Building of the Year Award, presented by the Royal Fine Art Commission Trust in 2002. McAllister's Fountain Pump House, adjacent to the Festival Grand Vista, houses powerful pumps for the restored fountain pool. The nearby lavatories were designed to be light and airy, with glass blocks, sunny colours and open ends to draw in fresh air. The Fountain Pump House and lavatories were awarded a commendation by the Civic Trust in 2006.

Day to day, the restoration project was run by Park Manager Jennifer Ullman and two landscape architects, Robert Wells and Graeme Rosser. Every detail of the designs and build was tested and scrutinised by Wells and Rosser. During the build, they were on site daily, checking every delivery, assessing loads of soil, monitoring the quality of the plants and meeting contractors to make sure costs stayed on budget.

The landscape restoration was designed by Hilary Taylor Landscape Associates (HTLA), a practice with a strong track record in the restoration of historic parks and gardens. Hilary Taylor conducted extensive research into the Park's history, using historic plans, plant lists, photographs and postcards to piece together lost landscape features. Archaeology was commissioned for the Subtropical Gardens, identifying planting bed sites and seeking to confirm the innovative construction of the substructure of the beds.

Despite having more than £10 million to spend, the team quickly realised that there were insufficient funds to restore the entire Park, so decisions had to be taken as to which historic features to put back and which to omit. Funding was focused on the historic garden features, such as the Subtropical Garden, the Rosery Garden, the Festival of Britain Gardens and the Riverside Promenade. Additionally, much of the original perimeter planting and internal shrub beds were prioritised, with some 3,500 deciduous trees, 1,200 conifers and 26,000 shrubs sourced for the Park and grown on for more than a year by the nursery Tendercare.

A plant delivery

Before the restoration works began, a number of trees had to be felled, including a row of mature horse chestnuts on the Riverside which were losing branches through age and disease and had become dangerous. Also felled were trees that

Removal of Horse Chestnut trees on the riverside 2001

had been planted inappropriately in the 20th century in areas that were designed to be open and treeless.

In February 2001, forty acres on the northern side of the Park were closed, including North Carriage Drive, a favoured route for commuting cyclists. Balfour Beatty Construction Limited took possession of the site and work began. Prior to the restoration, the Riverside was a visual hodge-podge, with paths of different levels remaining from the Festival of Britain, and derelict bases of pavilions causing trip hazards in the lawn. The lamp columns lined the 1950s concrete wall, blocking the vistas of the river. The London Peace Pagoda had been built in the centre of the riverside landscape on flat turf, seemingly out of place in its surroundings

HTLA found original plans and drawings for the Riverside showing a broad promenade with planted alcoves, including designs by Pennethorne for an elegant granite wall with inset benches and drawings by Gibson for the planting, showing trees on top of undulating mounds. These features had never been built because

Riverside promenade pre-restoration with diseased Horse Chestnut trees and obtrusive lamp standards

Riverside promenade post-restoration with wide path and benches as intended by Pennethorne

of the high tides of the River Thames eroding this area of the Park in the 19th century. Given the amount of historical evidence for the design, the team decided to build a landscape as close to the original designers' intentions as possible.

Peter Vickers of HTLA designed the riverside wall formed in pre-cast concrete, and after many trials and much experimentation working with Evans Concrete he devised a system to attach it to the existing 1950s wall with the addition of railings to produce a safe height. Achieving the right colour and character, as well as dealing with the varying height and angles of the existing wall, proved a challenge but was ultimately successful. This innovative design won a concrete industry award and has since been used in other parts of London.

For the new wide paths, pink granite chippings were rolled into fibreglass to provide a hardwearing surface similar in colour to the gravel paths originally used in the Park. Great curving mounds topped with trees were formed to embrace the Peace Pagoda, with additional areas of ornamental bedding and a smooth new concrete prayer platform for ceremonial use. The lamp columns were moved to the opposite side of the path, as originally specified by Gibson, opening up vistas of Albert Bridge and across the river to Chelsea.

North Carriage Drive was resurfaced in hardwearing red tarmac, the pedestrian paths surfaced in compacted gravel with red-painted hoop-topped fencing and dark-green estate rail installed to protect newly planted areas. The colours were chosen to reflect the original colouring of the railings before the death of Prince Albert threw the nation into mourning and resulted in railings being painted black in most public parks.

To the south of the carriage drive were the semi-derelict remains of the Festival Gardens. The fountains of the Grand Vista could be run manually only for a few hours a week in the summer under the supervision of Park engineers. The remaining brick walls of the Russell Page Garden were crumbling and the garden had been bisected by a wide path linking the Pagoda to the Bandstand. Tennis courts had been built next to the British Genius Site on an area that had once been the heart of the Festival Gardens. All the original colourful planting by Russell Page had been lost.

Designing the restoration of the Festival Gardens was challenging as it was impossible to replace the original structures and pavilions that had made up so much of the vitality and colour of the Festival. Additionally, in the late 1990s and early 2000s, 1950s design was considered to be in poor taste, still too recent to be valued and its colourfulness regarded as garish. In the original bid to the Heritage Lottery Fund, a different design consultant had proposed removing the

Re-planting the Russell Page Garden

Page's vivid colour scheme re-created

remaining walls and railings of the Russell Page Garden and tracing the outlines of the Festival buildings in stone amongst grass, erasing all structures of the visual pageant that had once been there. Hilary Taylor argued persuasively that the 1950s era was as important as any part of the historic design of the Park and fortunately was able to persuade the Heritage Lottery Fund to support her approach.

The Russell Page Gardens were restored as faithfully as possible, rebuilding the retaining walls and reinstating the latticed planting beds with their jostling colour schemes. The new Tea Terrace, a decorative silhouette of the Tea Pavilion drawn in the air, was designed as a place where visitors could sit and enjoy the Festival Gardens whilst taking refreshment from the adjacent kiosk.

On the site of the Festival's enormous striped dance tent, the team designed a raised mound with vibrant stripes of colourful bedding flowers protected by whimsical railings with floating balls. Colour choices for all materials were taken

from the cover of the original 1951 Festival Pleasure Gardens Guide and other images from the Festival era to ensure they were as accurate as possible.

During the Festival of Britain, the end of the Grand Vista was finished with a cut-out of the facade of the Crystal Palace from which fireworks were let off every evening. Unable to recreate the structure for reasons of safety, the restoration team decided to mimic the outline of the Crystal Palace facade in water, with

powerful towers of water rising 46 feet (14 metres) into the sky. The wind from the jets carries a fine spray of water onto the concrete surround, and on sunny days this has become for many Park visitors a favourite place to get a soaking. The fountain jets are all now fully automated and run daily during the summer months.

Central Avenue was resurfaced with a reduced centre circle constructed around the repainted Bandstand with twenty-seven ornate cast-iron benches designed

from photographs of benches in the Park from the early 20th century. Railed, mounded shrubberies were established to reinstate the once exotic specimen plants of the 19th-century fledgling Park and to act as a transition between the Victorian and Festival landscape

In autumn 2003, the Restoration moved on to the Subtropical Garden. Archæol-

ogy and detailed research had revealed the location of the original island planting beds and decisions had to be made about the planting. In Gibson's day, large, tender plants were taken into glasshouses every winter for protection and returned to the Subtropical Garden in spring once all danger of frost had passed.

As the Park no longer had functioning greenhouses, the plants chosen needed

59

to be hardy year-round with minimal protection. Additionally, Gibson had used a great deal of carpet bedding in many of his beds. This is a labour-intensive style of bedding, and limitations in future maintenance budgets meant that it was impossible for this to be replicated. Choosing the hardiest plants available and restricting the areas of bedding to those with the greatest visual impact, the team designed planting schemes to echo the original visual effect, using large-leaved bananas, cannas, tree ferns and hardy palms.

Another garden area to be restored was the Rosery Garden, so named for the different kinds of roses grown within it. Photographs of the original garden were rare and the garden area had been absorbed into the Deer Enclosure when the latter was expanded in the 1980s. Taylor used guidance from original plans of the Park as well as archaeology to locate the original layout. As this was a formal garden linking the Queenstown Circus entrance with the wider landscape of the Park, she included cast-iron scroll-back benches and hoop-topped fencing. Shrub borders were reinstated along the Prince of Wales Drive boundary and car park. Wide beds of perennials were created along the south side of the Lake. Paths were resurfaced and new railings installed to protect the planting.

The Duke of Edinburgh with Chief Lola Ayonrinde, Mayor of Wandsworth

The restoration was opened by HRH The Duke of Edinburgh on 4 June 2004. Improvements did, however, continue beyond the restoration's completion. In the spring of 2004, the Friends of Battersea Park proposed a new garden for the area near Sun Gate known as the Heather Garden. The heathers had been planted on the mounded silt that had accumulated through dredging of the lake some years previously and they were failing due to the alkaline soil. The Friends pointed out that each generation had seen a new garden of significance created in the Park, citing the Subtropical Garden, the Old English Garden and the Festival of Britain Pleasure Gardens as examples. They urged that a new modern garden be created,

designed by one of the great garden designers of the day. The Friends further stipulated that it should be designed to be colourful in winter, when most of the Park was bleak and grey.

Dan Pearson, an internationally renowned designer and plantsman, was chosen to develop a plan for the Garden. The resulting design celebrates winter with a rich selection of plants that come into their own between leaf-drop and budburst. Evergreens are contrasted with deciduous plants chosen for their bark, winter colour, interesting form and leaf structure, and scent. Ribbons of bulbs flow through the space, with different moods created in different areas by the plants. At the centre is a restful lawn and seating area around a stand of Persian Iron-wood trees (*Parrotia persica*). It is a tranquil space with year-round interest as well as delicate winter beauty, from the 'light entrance' of silver birches to the 'dark exit' with evergreens. The garden is a triumph for the Friends of Battersea Park, who raised funds tirelessly for five years to see it completed. The Winter Garden was opened on 3 March 2011 by the Mayor of London, Boris Johnson.

Persian Ironwood tree

A further garden that saw improvement at this time was the Old English Garden. In1998, to celebrate their 10th Anniversary, the Friends sponsored a new fountain, copying the original Edwardian fountain from photographs. Since 2009, Thrive has been the custodian of the Old English Garden, turning a once neglected space into a garden that provides horticultural training and therapy to trainee gardeners

living with physical disabilities or mental ill health. With the support of Sarah Price, another renowned designer, the Old English Garden has been transformed with a new perennial planting scheme that echoes its Arts and Crafts past, with old-fashioned shrub roses, honeysuckle and jasmine planted in abundance. Long flowering white valerian (*Centranthus ruber* 'Alba'), purple sage (*Salvia nemorosa*) and pink geranium (*Geranium* 'Patricia') create visual links across the garden.

As with all landscapes, Battersea Park continues to change with time. New projects are developed to improve the Park, and some areas inevitably decline through competition for decreasing maintenance funds. Weather conditions also have an impact, frosting borderline hardy plants in the Subtropical Garden, or depriving long-established trees of sufficient water to survive. These cycles of improvement and decline have taken place in the Park for the last 150 years and will continue to do so. However, 21st-century Park users are enjoying the benefits of a quarter of a century of progress and will be the next generation to champion its further protection and development.

The Rosery Garden

Sculpture

Some of the finest outdoor sculptures in London can be found in Battersea Park, including works by Henry Moore and Barbara Hepworth, part of the long association that the Park has had with the arts. The earliest surviving sculpture is the 24th Infantry Division War Memorial by Eric Kennington (1888–1960), which stands near the junction of Central Avenue and East Carriage Drive. Three tall men wearing uniform and carrying rifles stride over a serpent entwined around their legs. Below them on a tall, cylindrical plinth are the embossed badges of the units of the Division.

Kennington was born in Chelsea and served in the First World War as a private with the 13th London Regiment, the Kensingtons. Invalided out in 1915, he spent his convalescence painting *The Kensingtons at Laventie*, which, when exhibited for the benefit of the Star & Garter Building Fund, caused a sensation. Depicting a group of men standing exhausted under the weight of their equipment in a destroyed village, it is a moving tribute to the ordinary soldier. Appointed an official war artist, Kennington was asked to recommend a sculptor to commemorate the Division's 10,865 dead. Despite never having sculpted before, he immediately volunteered himself, refusing to take any payment for the work, in which he was assisted by Lucy Sampson from the Royal College of Art, who carved the badges. Kennington created a testimony to the courage and youth of the infantry. From left to right, the figures are based on Trooper Morris Clifford Thomas of the Machine Gun Corps, Sergeant J. Woods of the 9th Royal Sussex, and the poet Robert Graves, who served as a captain with the 2nd Battalion of the Royal Welch Fusiliers. The last two are depicted holding hands, which caused some controversy at the time.

The Memorial was unveiled in October 1924 by Field Marshal Lord Plumer and the Bishop of Southwark. At the dedication, Kennington explained: '… all three men have boundless strength, courage and resolve and their progress is unimpeded by the common danger at their feet – the enemies which they overcome are not so much German soldiers as the internal enemies of all of us.'

THREE STANDING FIGURES
HENRY MOORE
...TED TO THE LCC BY THE CONTEMPORARY ART...

In 1948, the first of a series of large international exhibitions of modern sculpture was held in the Park in the sheltered grass area where the Subtropical Garden had been. Organised by the London County Council (LCC) in association with the Arts Council, these exhibitions profiled works from the previous fifty years but – as Nikolaus Pevsner wrote in the introduction to the 1951 Exhibition – the works came from three generations of artists representing different movements: the realism of Rodin's era, the influence of Impressionism on artists such as Maillol, and the sculptural reactions to Cubism and Abstraction in the works of Henry Moore and Barbara Hepworth. Further exhibitions were held in 1960, 1963 and 1966. They included work by the finest international sculptors and by British sculptors such as Jacob Epstein and Elisabeth Frink.

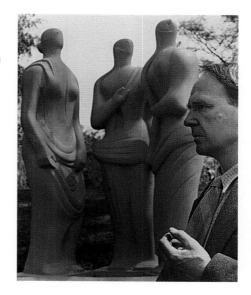

During the 1948 exhibition, the Contemporary Art Society offered Henry Moore's *Three Standing Figures* to the LCC so that it might be given a 'permanent and honoured place in one of the London Parks'. The notes of the Joint Establishment and Parks Committees on 17 and 18 June 1948 welcoming the donation state that the Museum of Modern Art in New York had wanted the finished work, as the group of figures had been recognised as one of the artist's greatest achievements, but that the Society was anxious that the group should remain in the UK. The present site of the sculpture by the lake was agreed with Henry Moore, who visited the Park. Describing his work and its background in his sketches of people in air-raid shelters, Moore said:

'The three figures were sited where they were shown in the first open air sculpture exhibition at Battersea Park, but they couldn't remain there because the tree to the right of one of them was rotten, and after it was felled the site lost a good deal of its attractiveness. But I was very happy about that original situation. The slight rise overlooking an open stretch of park and the background of trees emphasised their outward and upward stare into space. They are the expression in sculpture of the group feeling that I was concerned with in the shelter drawings, and although the problem of relating separate sculptural units was not new to me, my previous experience of the problem had involved more abstract forms; the bringing together of these three figures involved the creation of a unified human mood. The pervading theme of the shelter drawings was the group sense of communion in the three figures ... I wanted to overlay it with the sense of release, and create figures conscious of being in the open air, they have a lifted gaze, for scanning distances.'

Some of the press at the time were less than complimentary. An article in the *Daily Telegraph* of 22 June 1950 about the unveiling stated: 'It is a modernist conception of three women, having emerged from an air-raid shelter in various stages of bewilderment and undress, staring vacantly into the skies. It aroused considerable controversy when it was first displayed'.

The other great sculpture that remains from the exhibitions in the Park is Barbara Hepworth's *Single Form (Memorial)*, which was a tribute to her friend Dag Hammarskjöld, Secretary General of the United Nations (1953–61), who was killed in an air crash on 18 September 1961. The piece is a ten-foot-high abstract bronze figure, with a hole pierced through one side of the upper form. Hammarskjöld had been in discussion with Hepworth about a large-scale work for the United Nations at the time of his death and he may have been aware of the concept for the piece, possibly having seen an earlier version carved in wood, now at Tate St Ives. On Hammarskjöld's death, Hepworth was driven to create the piece in bronze. She said: '... when I heard of his death, in a kind of despair, I made the ten-foot high *Single Form (Memorial)... Memorial* was made just to console myself, because I was so upset'.

The sculpture was exhibited in Battersea Park in the summer of 1963 in the Subtropical Garden as part of *Sculpture: Open-Air Exhibition of Contemporary British and American Works*, and was then moved, at Hepworth's request, to its permanent site facing the Henry Moore across the lake. Hepworth developed *Single Form* into a much bigger version sited in front of the UN building in New York, where it serves as a permanent memorial to Hammarskjöld.

Of the many sculptures permanently on display in the Park, *Monument to the Brown Dog*, better known as *The Little Brown Dog*, is probably least familiar because of its peaceful location on the Woodland Walk next to the Old English Garden.

University College students demonstrate against the original brown dog statue, 1906

Unveiled on 12 December 1985, *The Little Brown Dog,* by sculptor Nicola Hicks (b.1960), is a reinterpretation of an earlier statue of a little brown dog with a controversial history.

The original statue was installed in 1906 in Latchmere Recreation Ground, a small community space south of Battersea Park. Sponsored by anti-vivisection organisations, the Brown Dog Memorial commemorated the treatment of a small brown terrier that had been the victim of prolonged vivisection experiments, the subject of which was at the centre of a trial for libel brought by Dr William Bayliss of University College London against Mr Stephen Coleridge of the National Anti-Vivisection Society. Coleridge had labelled Bayliss a torturer, while Bayliss maintained that his actions were within the terms of his licence for medical research. Bayliss won, but the publicity around the case was enormous, and the newspapers launched a campaign to raise funds to pay Coleridge's fine. More money than the fine was raised, and this was used to pay for the statue.

From its unveiling, the 1906 statue was the focus of protest. Defenders of vivisection thought the inscription on the statue was as libellous as Coleridge's original accusations. The statue was attacked repeatedly, so that 24-hour police protection was required. In 1910, after months of wearying debate, Battersea Borough Council decided to remove the statue as maintaining its security was proving too expensive. On 19 March 1910, 3,000 protesters marched from Hyde Park Corner to Trafalgar Square to protest against its removal, but to no avail. In 1911, the Council ordered that the Brown Dog Memorial be destroyed.

The 1985 statue was commissioned by the National Anti-Vivisection Society and the British Union for the Abolition of Vivisection. Originally next to the Pump House, the statue was moved to its current position in 1994 following the refurbishment of the Pump House as a Gallery.

The original inscription on the 1906 statue appears on one side of the plinth:

> In Memory of the Brown Terrier Dog
> Done to Death in the Laboratories of
> the University College in February 1903
> after having endured Vivisection extending
> over more than Two Months and having
> been handed over from one Vivisector to
> Another Till Death came to his Release.
>
> Also in Memory of the 232 dogs Vivisected
> at the same place during the year 1902.
>
> Men and women of England,
> how long shall these things be?

Little Brown Dog continues to evoke strong emotions and is regularly decorated with ribbons and flowers.

Steve Bunn, Roller Coaster

In 1996, in recognition of the Park's history of displaying great sculpture, the Friends of Battersea Park decided to launch an annual Sculpture Award, where the work of a talented young sculptor would be displayed for a year. Originally a wide competition, after the first few years the Friends decided to limit the call for sculptures to the students of the Royal College of Art's Sculpture School following its relocation to Hester Road in Battersea. The brief of creating a work that will stand up to a park environment, with changeable weather and curious visitors, has sometimes proved too challenging for the piece to survive the year.

However, notable successes have included Steve Bunn's 1999 *Roller Coaster,* an exuberant large-scale work created for the site outside the Pump House Gallery. This led to a commission for Bunn to make a work for the Millennium Dome and he went on to become a tutor at the Sculpture School. In 2007, Maxine Schaffer created *The Big Weed – Buckhorn Plantain* for the Sculpture Award. A large metal

The Millennium Cross

The Anzac Memorial

Maxine Schaffer, The Big Weed - Buckhorn Plantain
and Michael Pecirno, The Air Above, *winner of the 2014 Sculpture prize*

cut-out of a plant painted orange, the work was hung on the side of the Millennium Arena and by common consensus remained in place after the year ended – the only work created for the contest to do so. Other sculptures in the Park are the *Millennium Cross* at the western end of Central Avenue, donated to mark the Millennium in 2000, and the *Anzac Memorial,* at the eastern end of Central Avenue, donated by News Corporation, also in 2000.

Sport

What do Prince William, David Beckham and Bob Marley have in common? Or Sebastian Coe, Greg Rusedski and William Hague? They have all played, trained or been spectators at sporting events in Battersea Park. Through sport, the Park contributes to the health and wellbeing of thousands of people. Many are content with a brisk walk, but others run, play tennis, hockey, football, rugby, cricket or bowls, or take part in one of the many fundraising charity runs.

The Santa Run raising funds for Home Start, *a childen's charity*

The Park has had a role in the history of sport-related fundraising. An estimated £10 million is raised for charity each year through events in the Park, many of which focus on sports. The largest is the J.P. Morgan Chase Corporate Challenge, a 5.6km run which takes place over two evenings each July. In 2013, 26,675 runners including Olympic Gold rower Katherine Grainger took part, raising money for the charity Water Aid. In 1994, the first Race for Life event was held in the Park to support cancer research. Some 750 participants raised £48,000. In 2013, the charity ran the event nationwide and raised more than £50 million.

Battersea Park.

Sidders
Series

When the Park was laid out in the 1850s, there was a 'cricket match ground' and two 'practice grounds', which were informal grass sports pitches for multiple uses. In the very early days, these and other open grass areas were 'mown' by sheep. There was also a gymnasium in the south-west corner of the Park, boating on the lake and ice-skating on Ladies Pond.

Across London, sports grounds were being built to meet the growing demand for recreation. This partly originated from the Temperance Movement, which looked for healthy activities for factory workers' leisure time, but was also meant to meet the needs of a growing middle class of office workers for whom sport was believed to teach morality, strengthen character and provide an invigorating antidote to sedentary work. Changes in working patterns by the 1880s had created more leisure time and opportunities for sport, with most industries moving towards an eight-hour day and some offices and factories closing on Saturday afternoons.

Battersea Park is well known for its contribution to the history of football. In the mid-19th century, football had no official set of rules and was a far more violent game than it is today. There were no referees, tackling was vicious, and in some versions of the game there was unrestricted use of hands on the ball. In an attempt to invest the sport with fairness and to end disputes about how it should be played, a group of team captains and secretaries came together in October 1863 to decide on a set of rules. This was the formation of the Football Association. Decisions on the final set of rules took several more meetings, but on 9 January 1864 the first official game following Football Association rules was played in Battersea Park. This is commemorated by a plaque on the sports pavilion, unveiled in 2014 on the 150th anniversary of the original game.

Football has remained popular ever since. With new rules and agreement on pitch size, the football fields in the Park became more established, being mown and marked out for matches. The need for a more weatherproof surface led to the creation of the all-weather balls games area in 1939. This remains one of the busiest areas of the Park, with schools and clubs playing football and hockey throughout the year on pitches that can be floodlit to allow evening play. Since

the early 21st century the Park has had a close relationship with the Chelsea Football Club, which provides holiday and summer football training schemes for local children.

In the 1880s, a craze for cycling developed in Battersea Park. The penny-farthing had been replaced by the 'safety bicycle', which had front and back wheels of the same size and pneumatic tyres. Baroness Orczy wrote:

'Directly after its introduction, bicycling at once became not only of general utility to women, but also very fashionable. In the late 'nineties the great thing in London was to go and watch the bicycling in Battersea Park. After tea-time the Park was thronged with all the smartest women in London'.

Battersea was chosen as the place to be as the Carriage Drives were hard-packed, which provided a good surface, and Hyde Park did not then allow cycling. In the early 20th century, women cyclists adopted 'bloomers'. These were loose, skirt-like trousers secured at the ankles, which had caused great controversy

Cyclists in Battersea Park *from* The Sketch, *24 July 1895*

when first pioneered in England in the 1890s. The magazine *Punch* published a letter in 1895 from 'Arry', a fictitious cockney social commentator, about 'them beauties on bikes':

So they straddle the bike ah la Brixton, and
    tumble to Battersea Park.
'Dividers' and 'Knickers' my Dysy, are
    sniffed at out Hislington way,
But when countesses mount 'em at Chelsea,
    they're trotty and puffeck OK!

World shifts it, old man, that's a moral!
    We'll soon 'ave some duchess, on wheels,
A-cuttin' all records, and showing young
    ZIMMY a clean pair of 'eels'.

Cycling remains very popular, with *London Recumbents* hiring out a range of unusual cycles to people of all ages and abilities.

Once the management of the Park had passed to the London County Council (LCC) in 1889, the emphasis on sport increased. This was largely due to the development of new rules for games, including for pitch sizes and surface finishes, plus the requirement for changing rooms. In the 1880s and 1890s the number of sports facilities grew, with the addition of a bowling green and grass tennis courts. A new boat house was built in 1909 and a cycle shelter in 1913. Paddling pools were added in 1922. The all-weather pitch, hard-surfaced tennis courts, a putting green and the running track with its pavilion were all installed before the Second World War.

James Wallace 1872-1911, *A Game of Tennis in Battersea Park*, 1904

In the early days, there were three outdoor gyms in the Park, separated into areas for men, women and children. Although no photographs of the three outdoor gyms survive, a contemporary description suggests what they might have been like:

> Almost every big park has a public gymnasium, the apparatus being specially arranged to meet the differing requirements of children, youths and adults. Thus no one under 12 is allowed in the "seniors" part, while no one over that age may make use of the juvenile division. In the latter swings and see-saws predominate, whereas the rings, giant-strides, climbing ropes and poles are always confined to the former section. ... A curious fact in connection with these park gymnasia is that, although the floor is generally composed of asphalt, accidents are extremely rare

There is an outdoor fitness trail now, which is very popular, but from the above description, the children's gymnasium with its swings and see-saws can be seen as a direct precursor of the modern-day playground. Playgrounds were first created to give children somewhere to learn fair play in a safe environment, and the main playground in Battersea Park has undergone many changes and refurbishments over the years as play equipment wears out and theories and regulations of play change. Both the much loved Adventure Playground and the One O'Clock Club for children aged under-5, closed in 2013 due to Wandsworth Council budget cuts. A new free, less adventurous playground opened on the site in 2014, and in 2015 *Go-Ape* opened a tree top adventure course, run from what used to be the Adventure Playground building. Also in 2015 *Putt in the Park* opened a café and putting green in the space previously occupied by the One O'Clock Club.

Go-Ape treetop adventure course

Putt in the Park café and putting green

In the 1880s and 1890s new sports became popular, including netball and tennis. Netball owes its origin to basketball, but was a non-contact version of the sport, so was deemed acceptable for women, as were croquet and tennis. In 1874, the first attempt was made to standardise the rules of tennis and the layout of the court. Struggling to find suitable places to play, people quickly realised that croquet lawns, with their smooth grass surfaces, were widely available and perfect for tennis. The popularity of tennis led to the first hard-surfaced tennis courts being constructed in the Park in 1924. Today there are nineteen floodlit tennis courts that remain busy throughout the year, some of which are also used for netball.

During the Second World War, the athletics track was used as an anti-aircraft rocket battery, from which rockets were fired at aircraft during bombing raids. The athletics pavilion served as the railway station for the *Far Tottering and Oyster Creek Railway* during the Festival of Britain. It then reverted to its original use as a popular athletics training centre until it was demolished before the construction in 1999 of the new Millennium Arena. This was designed to be a centre for sporting excellence, with a competition-level running track and athletics facilities, a gym, tennis courts and astro-turf sports areas with markings for football and hockey. The Millennium Arena was declared open on 1 June 2000 by the 1984 Olympic Javelin Champion Tessa Sanderson CBE, who trained for six Olympics in the Park and subsequently coached young athletes there.

The Millennium Arena Galleries

From its early beginnings as a home for sport, the Park has seen the introduction of many new forms of recreation. From boot-camp-style fitness classes to tai-chi, skateboarding, fishing, pilates and boules, today's Park offers opportunities for sport for every age, ability and level of fitness.

85

For many years Battersea Park was a regular home to large public parades, most notably the Easter Parade. More recently events such as Vintage and Classic cars and carriages and the London Harness Horse Parade have been staged.

In June 2015 the first race to be held in England for Formula E electrically powered racing cars took place over two days on a specially created circuit on the existing carriageways of the Park. The event caused the Park to be significantly disrupted for three weeks and effectively closed to park users for four days over the race. It excited great controversy amongst local residents as to its appropriateness as an event in the Park. The Council agreed for it to continue with some amendment for 2016 and many people greatly fear it will become an annual event.

Gibson's Order to Veitch's Nursery dated 19 Aug 1882

Flora and Fauna

After 150 years of growth, the older trees of Battersea Park are majestic specimens, fulfilling John Gibson's vision of an arboretum-style landscape full of interest and variety.

The mid-19th century was a time of great botanical discovery as the British Empire expanded across the globe. Private nurseries, such as James Veitch & Son were quick to realise the commercial potential of selling exotic plants to the growing middle class. In its heyday, Veitch's sent twenty-two plant-hunters abroad to collect exclusively for its nursery. Previous plant-hunting expeditions had been largely for the benefit of a few wealthy private sponsors and the government. A former plant-hunter himself, Gibson was keen to use as many new discoveries as possible in the Park.

Drawing on his extensive knowledge of rare plants and his network of horticultural contacts, Gibson bought trees from well-known plant-hunting nurseries including Veitch's and Waterer's. The newly sourced trees and shrubs would have been planted as small, twiggy specimens, as many of the parent plants had only recently been introduced into the UK. Eager to display these novelties to their best advantage, Gibson set them on mounds to make them look more impressive. Choice specimens were positioned at the junctions of paths, allowing them to be viewed from all angles and enticing visitors to continue with the promise of further excitements ahead.

The best place to see this is where the paths meet at the end of Ladies Pond close to the Subtropical Garden. The strawberry tree (*Arbutus x andrachnoides*), with its graceful wide branches and cinnamon-coloured flaking bark, is likely to be the *Arbutus unedo* mentioned on Gibson's plant order from Veitch's Nursery. Planted on a steeply raised mound close to the path, it is easily visible from either path around Ladies' Pond. Nearby, at the path fork, are the magnificent swamp cypress (*Taxodium distichum*) and dawn redwood (*Metasequoia glyptostroboides*) trees that announce to visitors that this is no ordinary landscape, but an exotic garden with horticultural treats from distant lands.

90

Strawberry tree (*Arbutus x andrachnoides*)

Gibson's surviving order lists and correspondence provide a wonderful glimpse into his planting plans, with requests for up to 300 plants of any one variety at a time, mainly trees, or the shrubs that form the backbone of the boundary planting. However, he would sometimes order as few as six, or even one of something special. Gibson exchanged plants and letters on the suitability of plants for the

Swamp Cyprus *(Taxodium distichum)*

Dawn Redwood (*Metasequoia glyptostroboides*)

London Plane (*Platanus x hispanica*)

urban environment with Jean-Pierre Barillet-Dechamps, the 'Jardinier en chef' of the parks service in Paris, describing favourite plants such as Persian lilac, Japanese privet, 'shrubs with distinctive foliage, aucuba, gold striped holly, rhododendron, planted in line in contrast with other plants in various shades of green'.

Some of Gibson's trees have been lost to old age and disease, but many new trees were planted as part of the restoration of the Park. Using Gibson's lists as guidance and keeping to Victorian principles of shrub planting, many thousands of plants at a cost of nearly £500,000 were sourced to reinstate the framing boundary planting and shrubberies, the specimen trees on the riverside, and the Sub-tropical and Rosery Gardens. A blend of evergreen plants for structure, such as holly and laurel, mixed with deciduous plants including spiraea and buddleia, create interest throughout the year. Rarities were planted amidst more common plants to echo Gibson's intention that the Park should be an arboretum of interesting varieties.

93

The Grace Darling memorial oak (*Quercus cerris*)

Over the years a number of trees have been planted celebrating extraordinary people or events, including the Grace Darling memorial oak (*Quercus cerris*) planted on the riverside in 1934, the semicircle of Pride of India trees (*Koelreuteria paniculata*) planted near West Carriage Drive in 1997 to commemorate fifty years since Indian Independence, the Maple Tree Leaf walk planted in 2008 with Canadian maples (*Acer rubrum*) and the Black Poplar *(Populus Nigra)* planted near Albert Bridge to celebrate the Queen's Diamond Jubilee in 2012.

The Park is home to approximately 4,000 trees with 172 named species. The most common of these is the London plane (*Platanus x hispanica*) followed by hollies, maples, limes and members of the prunus family. There is inevitably a cycle of change each year as some trees mature or become diseased, with a few being removed and new ones planted.

At first glance, the Park seems to be mainly grass areas with shrub borders and trees. But, tucked away, more colourful planting can be found: the Subtropical Garden with its giant-leaved plants and colourful underplanting; the Grand Vista and Russell Page Gardens, featuring vibrant bedding displays and roses; the Staff Yard, which has a herb garden and greenhouse, transformed by Thrive into a colourful oasis; and the Old English Garden and the Winter Garden, which have become star attractions through the introduction of new planting schemes.

Despite the emphasis on ornamental planting and great plant species from abroad, the Park is a haven for wildlife, with a wide variety of habitats, including the lake and the wooded areas on the east side of the Park, which have been managed specifically for wildlife since the late 1980s. These days, it is recognised that the entire Park is important to nature and it is managed accordingly.

William Bell Scott 1811-90. *Grace Darling and her father save survivors from the wreck of the steamer 'Forfarshire' on the Farne Rocks, Northumberland, 7 September 1838.*

The lake is host to a variety of bird species and famous for its heronry in the tall trees on the islands and surrounding banks. Black cormorants can be seen with their wings spread wide to dry after diving for fish. There are many varieties of duck, including mallard, pochard, tufted ducks and gadwall, as well as great crested grebes, moorhens and coots. Mute swans nest on the main lake in most years, fiercely defending their territory. Canada geese threatened to overwhelm the Park in the 1990s but numbers are now tightly controlled, greatly to the benefit of other species.

Across the Park, the raucous calls of the bright-green ring-necked parakeets can be heard as they fly in groups from tree to tree. They were unknown in Central London until their first breeding as domestic escapees in the Richmond area in the 1960s. Arriving in Battersea in the early 2000s, they are now widespread in the capital.

Ubiquitous birds include magpies, pigeons and crows. Less easily spotted birds making their home in the Park include dunnocks, goldcrests and tawny owls. A number of rarer birds pause for a short time during migration.

Great Crested Grebe
with young aboard

Coot with chick

Egyptian Goose
with goose-stepping youngster
(colloquially known as a 'humbug')

Shelduck

Pochard

Foxes breed in the Park and can occasionally be heard barking at night. Grey squirrels are everywhere, cadging food from anyone willing to feed them or turning out the contents of the litter bins. Bats circle over the Lake, feeding on insects as they fly.

Despite the success of the many animal species that live in the Park, it is an environment that has been created by humans and it has to be managed to ensure that there is a balance between species. Invasive non-native species, such as Canada geese and terrapins, are actively controlled to limit population numbers to manageable levels, in accordance with best practice guidelines. This enables a balance to be achieved across all the species.

Great Spotted Woodpecker

Tawny Owlets

Green Ring-necked Parakeets

Sleepy Fox

Hedgehog

Wood Mouse

Grey Squirrel

Red eared Terrapins

Common Frog

Common Toad

The Future

All landscapes change with time, and parks are especially dynamic places. Trees mature and die, new planting schemes are created, and sports facilities evolve to meet changing needs. Every generation brings fresh interests or events that leave behind them a legacy of change. During the 20th century, two World Wars led to significant alterations in the Park's appearance and three different organisations managed the Park: the London County Council (1889–1965), the Greater London Council (1965–1986) and Wandsworth Borough Council (1986–), all leaving their mark.

The way the Park is maintained has also changed. Until the late 1980s, it was maintained by on-site gardeners who developed skills over the years and were responsible for specific areas. The age of competitive tendering brought a change: gardeners now worked under a large horticultural maintenance contract that serviced the entire borough.

In the autumn of 2015, the Park, along with all Leisure and Cultural services and all of the existing management staff and horticultural maintenance contracts, was transferred from the direct management of Wandsworth Borough Council to a newly formed charity, *Enable Leisure and Culture Services Limited*. This allows the services to benefit from the financial advantages of charitable status in a time of cuts in public sector funding. As with all of the previous alterations in management structure that the Park has experienced, it is likely that the public is largely unaware of the change as they come to use the Park on a day-to-day basis, as they continue to see the same people tending flower beds, or meet the same familiar faces serving at the coffee kiosk or at the Millennium Arena.

What does matter is the long-term investment in the Park as it hosts millions of visitors each year, with the inherent wear and tear that people enjoying themselves bring. It is the responsibility of each generation to make sure that the Park gets the best possible care: and the best way to do that is to get involved; to join

the Friends of Battersea Park; to become a volunteer gardener or just generally to make your voice heard.

The Park will continue to be a special place no matter who is in charge: couples will get engaged there, families will create priceless memories, athletes will achieve personal bests, and all against the quiet backdrop of beauty that has become a part of so many of our lives.

Snapshots

The next few pages provide an album of people and day to day activity which will be familiar to those fortunate to be regular visitors to the Park. For those who are not, we hope that they will be encouraged to share the abundant pleasures on offer.

Acknowledgements

This book has been the work of many people and I am grateful to everyone who contributed time, energy, photographs and advice to make it a reality. A huge thank you must go to the small group of people who met regularly to push the project forward: Mike Bates, Hallam Murray and Frances Radcliffe, each making their own special contribution, and John Commander who brought expertise, patience and skill to putting the book together.

Thanks also go to the following for their invaluable help: Claire Elliot, Sally Orman, Karen Horan, Catherine Lamb and Philip Wright from the Friends and Jerry Birtles, Simon Cooper-Grundy, Simon Ingyon, Paul McCue and Valerie Selby from Enable, previously Wandsworth Borough Council.

Illustrations have come from a wide variety of sources. Over the years, the Battersea Park office has accumulated a range of rare images, many of them represented here. The Wandsworth Heritage Library has been a great source of historic material, as has the archive assembled over many years by Mike Bates in his role as production editor of the Friends' magazine *Review*. Particular thanks are due to Loretta Powell who generously made freely available her files of wonderful photographs which bring the Park so vividly to life. Drew Bennellick, David Hills and Miranda Watkins also contributed images.

We have not been able to acknowledge all the individual illustrations used. Any errors or omissions will gladly be rectified in the next edition and on the Friends of Battersea Park website at www.batterseapark.org

Information on the sources of the quotations and a general bibliography can also be found on the Friends' website.